You will n~~ee~~d
and a dice ~~...~~
way to the planet ~~Threadneedle~~
Any number of adventures may
be encountered........

Go now... put on your spacesuits
and try to capture a spaceship.
May the Great Warthog be
with you and protect you from
the dreaded Zogs!

Copyright text and illustrations © 1990 Shoo Rayner
First published 1990 by Blackie and Son Ltd

British Library Cataloguing in Publication Data
Rayner, Shoo
Games from the 21st century.
1. Children's board games
    I. Title
        794
ISBN 0-216-92961-X

Blackie and Son Ltd
7 Leicester Place
London WC2H 7BP

Printed in Hong Kong

Jessica

Cholmondeley

for
Nina

Any similarity between anything in this book and real life
is not only coincidental .... it's really quite amazing too !!!

Twelve Thrilling Trans-Galactic Board Games

GAMES from the 21st CENTURY

Spatially integrated by Shoo Rayner

Blackie
London

SPACE PORT

Using a dice, counters and luck, make your way to the capsule on top of the rocket, which is to take you on your trans-galactic journey.

Start in the passport control office. Throw the dice and move the number of squares shown, following the numbers.

If you land on a square guarded by Zogs, miss a turn until they move away. If you land on a square with a security camera, you will have to run past it very quickly, so have another go. If you land on a black and yellow fuel tank, miss a go, as these tanks are full of very sensitive chemicals, which must not be disturbed!

When you reach the cabin of the space capsule, throw a six to blast off! Good luck.

MADE IT
THROW A SIX TO BLAST OFF!

FUEL STORE

XL4·5

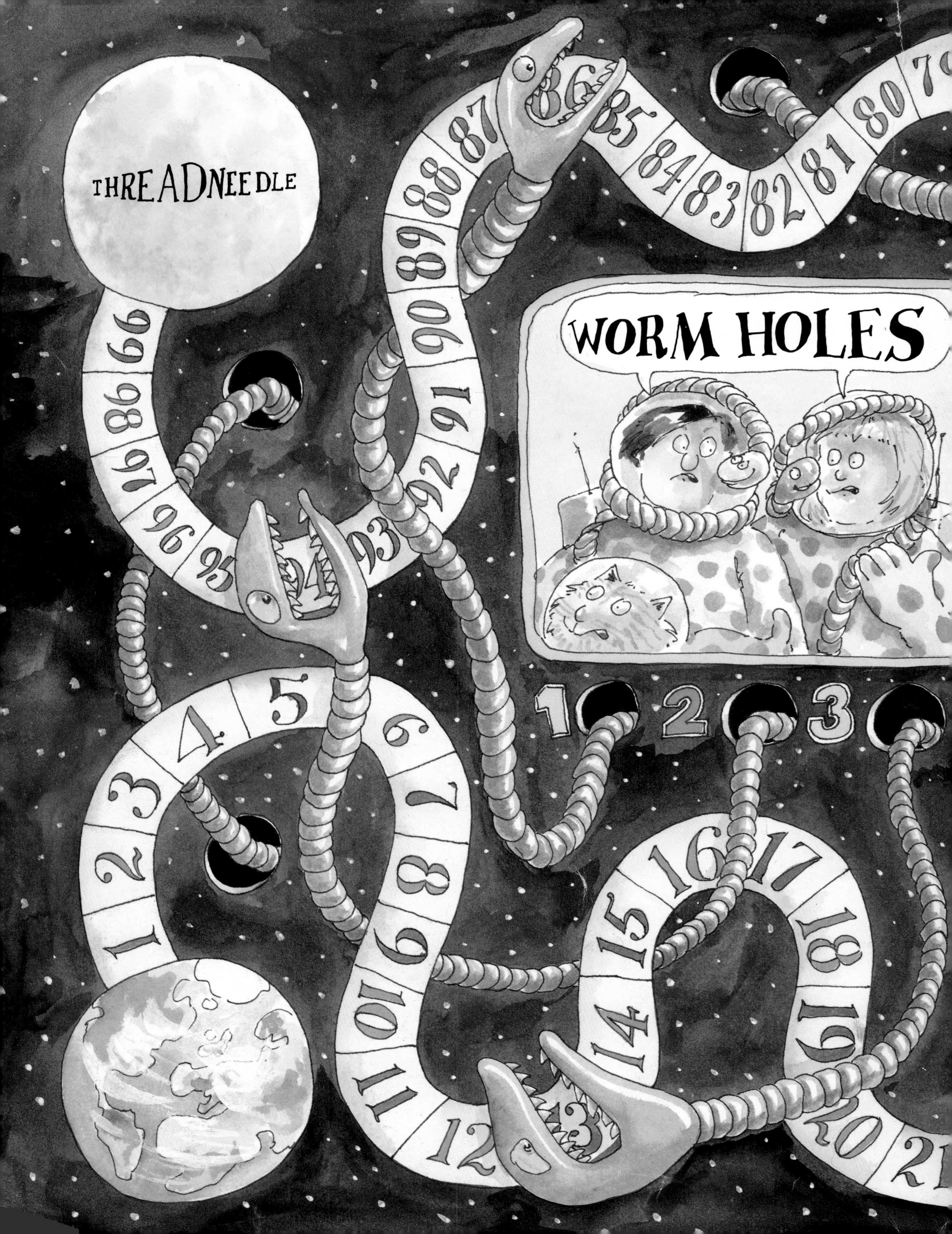
THREADNEEDLE
WORM HOLES
1
2
3

In the wild and woolly wastes of the eastern half of hyperspace lies the region of the Wormholes.

The worms can slow down, or speed up, your journey to the planet Threadneedle. If you land on the head of a worm, gravitational forces will drag you down to its tail and into the wormholes.

When you reach the wormholes, throw the dice again and come out of the wormhole with the same value as that on the dice, until you land on the head of the worm that lives in that hole.

The winner is the first to reach the planet Threadneedle.

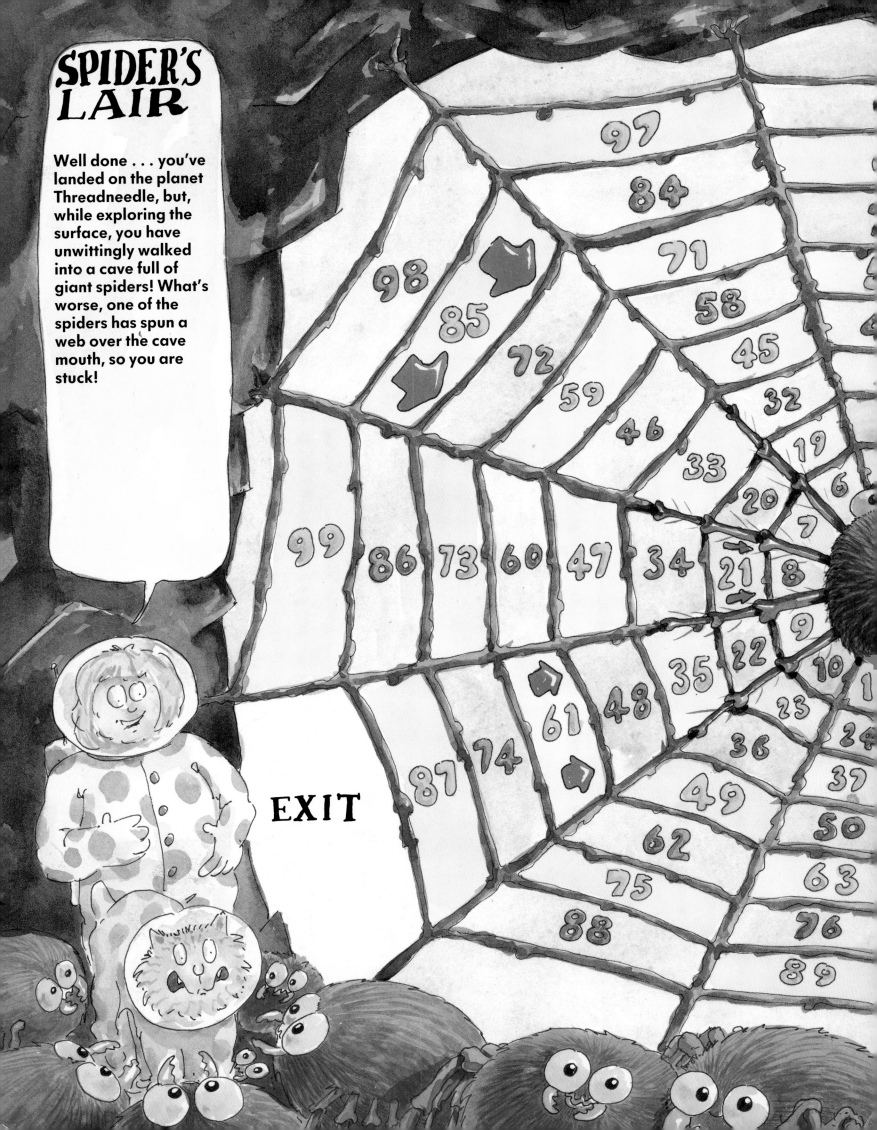

Start off on the spider's back in the middle of the web.

Work your way out towards the exit in an anti-clockwise fashion.

The spider can sense you moving on the squares with arrows in them. If you land on one of them, follow the arrows to the next square in. This may slow you down, but it's better than being eaten!

The winner is the first one out of the exit.

CRATER HOPPING

This is fun! There is low gravity on the planet Threadneedle so you can jump a lot further than on Earth.

At the start throw a 2, 3 or 6 and move to that crater. On your next go, throw the dice and move to the crater next to you with the same number.

ENTRANCE

START

PHORT NOQUES GALACTIC DEPOSITORY
This is the place. Start at entrance 1,2 or 3 by throwing that number on a dice. Or start from the entrance you finished at in 'CRATER HOPPING'.
At least there aren't any Zogs here. But it isn't going to be easy!
1
2
3
1
2
3
4
TAKE TUNNEL TO 16
5
20
ROBOT IN LIFT
MISS A GO
19
18
SECURITY ROBOT
MISS A GO
17
16
TAKE TUNNEL TO 4
21
22
23
TRANSMAT TO 33
24
25
TAKE TUNNEL TO 7
36
Lift waiting for you forward 2
35
34
33
TRANSMAT TO 16
32
37
38
39
TAKE TUNNEL TO 26
40
41

Work your way down to the central vault, following instructions on the way. Throw a six in square 28, or enter the vault in square 44. Keep going round the vault until you get hold of the tape of Ethyl and the Keytones, by landing on vault square 4.

If you land on vault square 5, you can throw a three to get out, otherwise you can go straight out of vault square 1.

The winner is the first to get out of the exits by throwing the exact score.

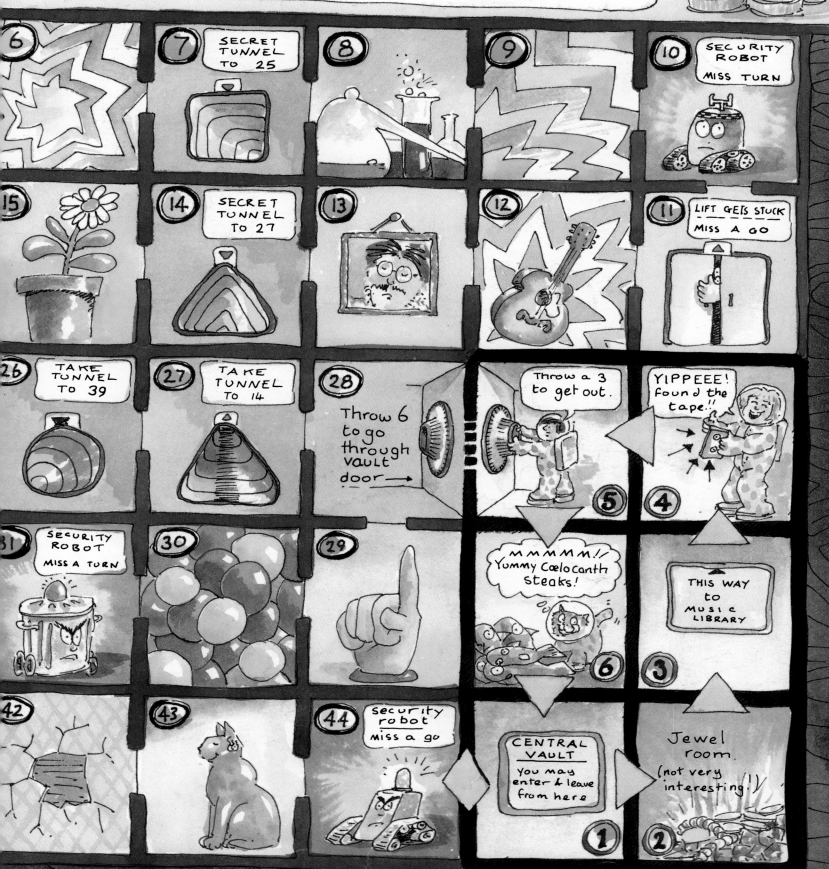

Thank heavens for the Throggles! Use them as stepping-stones to get across the swamp. You can move forward by the amount you have thrown on the dice.

Some of the Throggles are not having a good day. They have turned green. You will have to stop and listen to their problems for a while, so miss a go if you land on one. The red Throggles are having a really good day; they are so happy they bounce you on ahead, so if you land on one have another go.

The winner is the first back to the spaceship.

OUR COMPUTER'S GONE MAD!

Machines are not as reliable as Cats. (And that's a fact!)

The computer is full of Bugs! You will have to work your way to square 100 to clear the memory banks and reset the system. If you land on a bug square you will have to carry out the instructions given to you by the computer (written out below). If you can't – or won't – carry out the instructions, you will have to miss your next go.

The winner is the first to get to 100 and clean the screen.

2	Stand on one leg for a minute	54	Talk to your neighbour with a mouthful of water!
4	Go space walking	56	Do everyone's homework for them!
6	Forward 3	58	Back 1
8	Don't watch TV all day	60	Fly to Mars and back in three minutes
10	Don't blink for 30 seconds or miss a go	62	Do a handstand
12	Miss a turn	64	Catch Asteroids!
14	Tell the worst joke you know	66	Forward 1
16	Forward 5	68	Pay your left-hand neighbour a big compliment
18	Tell a whopping lie!	70	Make up a poem on a subject your neighbour gives you
20	Pretend you've been sick!	72	Tell a joke. Miss a go if it's not funny
22	Kiss your right-hand neighbour	74	Keep your room tidy for a week!
24	Throw again	76	Tell a shaggy dog story
26	Draw a picture of a space monster	78	Back 5
28	Go mad listening to Ethyl and the Keytones!	80	Don't make a noise for two minutes or miss a go
30	Back 3	82	Sing a sad song
32	Be teacher's pet all day!	84	Miss a turn
34	Tell the worst thing you ever did	86	Do the washing-up for a week
36	Sing a funny song	88	Tell the nicest thing you have ever done
38	Miss a turn	90	Play the rest of the game in slow motion
40	Make a drink for everyone	92	Move your neighbour's counter without them noticing!
42	Blow the biggest bubble-gum bubble in the Universe	94	Have a bit of a Byte to eat!
44	Back 3	96	Do whatever your left-hand neighbour asks! ! !
46	Tell a really good joke	98	Back 7
48	Forward 5	100	System cleared . . . . you're the winner!
50	Eat a dry biscuit and whistle!		
52	Miss a turn		

1 2 3 4 5 6 7 8 9 10
20 19 18 17 16 15 14 13 12 11
21 22 23 24 25 26 27 28 29 30
40 39 38 37 36 35 34 33 32 31
41 42 43 44 45 46 47 48 49 50
60 59 58 57 56 55 54 53 52 51
61 62 63 64 65 66 67 68 69 70
80 79 78 77 76 75 74 73 72 71
81 82 83 84 85 86 87 88 89 90
100 99 98 97 96 95 94 93 92 91

BLAST OFF

Oh dear! We forgot to switch off the spaceship's lights and now the batteries have run down. We will have to hunt around the planet for power crystals.

Throw the dice and move in the usual way. You cannot, however, simply move past a crystal square. Whenever you land on a crystal, stop and throw the dice again. If you throw the number on the crystal, you can claim it and throw again. If you don't throw the value of the crystal, you will have to wait your turn and try again. When you have picked up all the crystals, you can power up and be on your way.

The winner is the first to blast off.

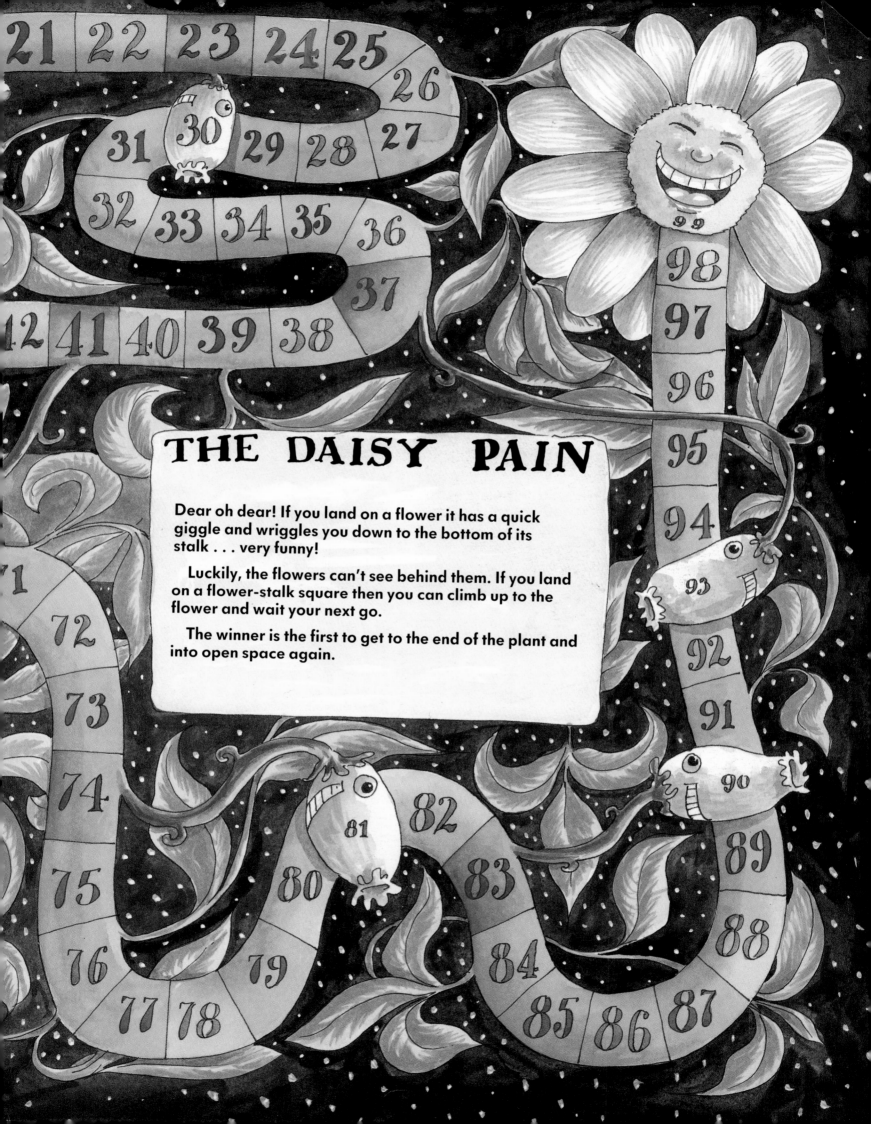

THE DAISY PAIN

Dear oh dear! If you land on a flower it has a quick giggle and wriggles you down to the bottom of its stalk . . . very funny!

Luckily, the flowers can't see behind them. If you land on a flower-stalk square then you can climb up to the flower and wait your next go.

The winner is the first to get to the end of the plant and into open space again.

BLACK HOLE AHEAD

The gravitational power of the Black Hole sucks you inexorably towards oblivion.

At the red flash co-ordinates on your inward spiral, you encounter RPQ's (Reverse Polarity Quirks!) which, if you land on them, throw you into the inner lane from yours and change your direction. If you land in the Black Hole (47) you must reconstitute yourself at the beginning and start again! Always follow the direction of the track you are on. The winner is the first to get themselves into Earth orbit.

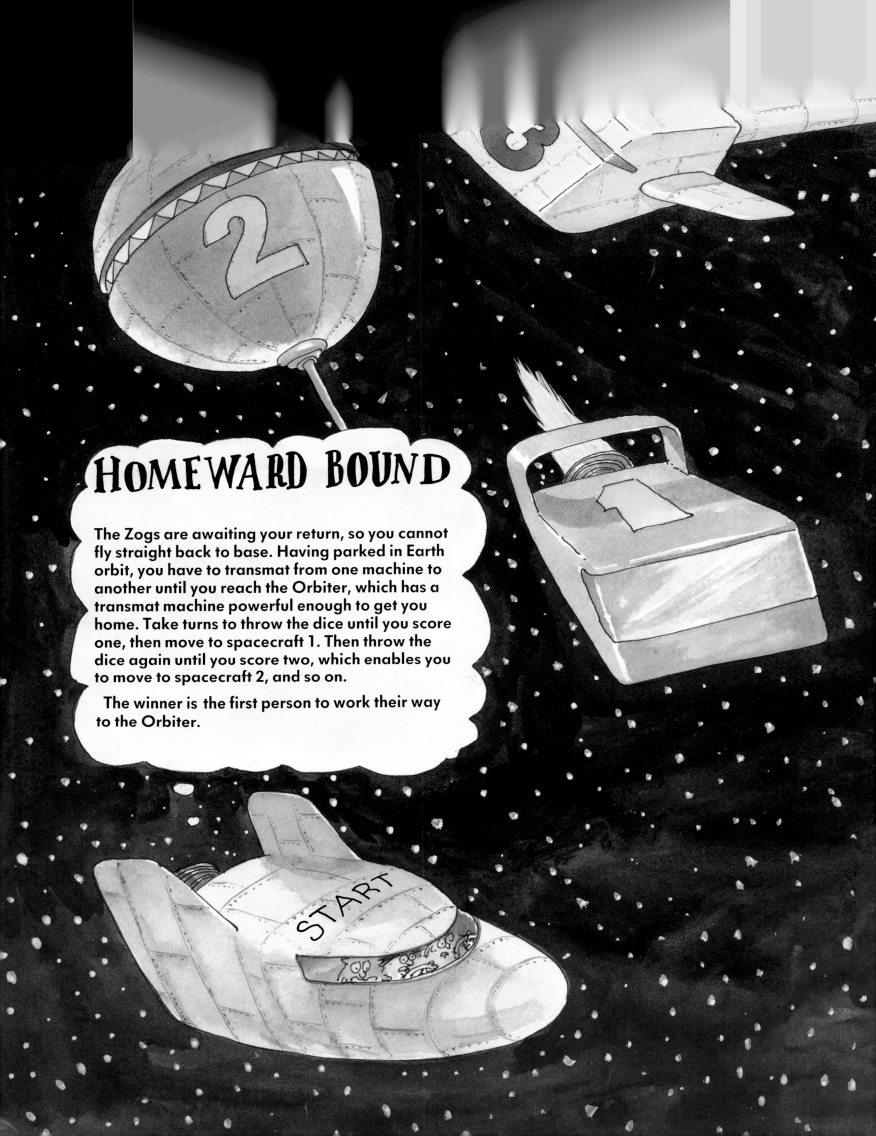

HOMEWARD BOUND

The Zogs are awaiting your return, so you cannot fly straight back to base. Having parked in Earth orbit, you have to transmat from one machine to another until you reach the Orbiter, which has a transmat machine powerful enough to get you home. Take turns to throw the dice until you score one, then move to spacecraft 1. Then throw the dice again until you score two, which enables you to move to spacecraft 2, and so on.

The winner is the first person to work their way to the Orbiter.